AMAZiNG ME!

A BOOK OF YOUR OWN WORLD RECORDS

written by James Buckley, Jr.

studio fun BOOKS

White Plains, New York • Montréal, Québec • Bath, United Kingdom

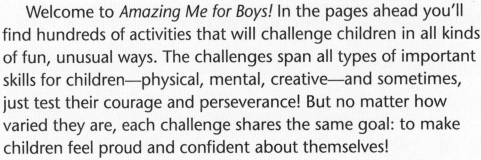

PARENT NOTE:
An Amazing Note to Adults!

Welcome to *Amazing Me for Boys!* In the pages ahead you'll find hundreds of activities that will challenge children in all kinds of fun, unusual ways. The challenges span all types of important skills for children—physical, mental, creative—and sometimes, just test their courage and perseverance! But no matter how varied they are, each challenge shares the same goal: to make children feel proud and confident about themselves!

Not every challenge is well-suited for every child. So we encourage you to get involved with your children as they use this book. Help them choose those challenges that best stretch their abilities and will most make them feel proud. With so many challenges to choose from, you're certain to find positive activities to keep any child busy for many months ahead!

A note about safety: If you ask someone to set a personal record, it's natural that they will push themselves hard. And that can create safety risks, no matter how simple the challenge. *Amazing Me!* books include a warning to children to ALWAYS be safe. As an adult, we ask that you supervise your child and reinforce this message, over and over! These challenges are first and foremost about fun. By keeping the focus there, we are certain that every single challenge will be a positive, laugh-filled experience!

Amazingly yours,

The Editors

TABLE OF CONTENTS

BE AMAZING!
HOW AMAZING ARE YOU?
THIS BOOK GIVES YOU THE CHANCE TO FIND OUT!

One way to show how amazing you are is to set world records… lots of them! Around the world, people try to gain fame and break barriers by setting world records. It's not just "how fast can you run 100 meters," but everything under the sun. There are world records in thousands of categories, from collecting baseballs to making giant pizzas to doing push-ups with one arm.

Now it's time for you to join the ranks…with this book full of challenges designed to prove how radically awesome you are! How many words can you say during one long belch? How fast can you write your name while holding the pencil with your toes? How high can you build a tower of playing cards? You might be surprised!

So fill in the blanks…do your best…and you'll be the proud holder of dozens of world records—until you break them yourself!

Safety First!

You can't set personal records if you don't try hard. But far more important than setting a record is being safe and having fun. So be sensible! Make sure your parents know what you are doing and ask for their help. Be smart, have fun, and don't do ANYTHING that will put you at risk of injury, or that can cause damage. Don't do anything you or your parents are not comfortable with. Remember—fun and laughs are the real goal!

MEASURING SUCCESS

Records have to be measured. You need to end up with a result. In this book, you'll measure a lot of different things. Here are some things you might want to keep handy:

- a stopwatch or a watch with a second hand (many phones have stopwatches on them, too)
- a measuring tape
- a scale for measuring weights
- your fingers (great for helping to count things!)
- a notebook to keep track of things that don't fit in here!
- a friend or two!

Measuring Strings
To measure long distances, here's a cool trick. Get a ball of thick string. Using a yardstick or measuring tape, measure a foot of the string and make a mark on it. Then, along the string's length, keep measuring feet and making marks. You can then use that marked-up string as a way to measure enormously long distances!

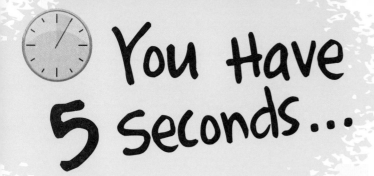

You Have 5 Seconds...

For each of these challenges, you get only five seconds! Start counting now: One-Mississippi, two-Mississippi, three-Mississippi... or get a friend to help you count!

IN A SNAP!

How many times can you snap your fingers in five seconds? Now try it with your other hand!

First Attempt: _____

My Amazing World Record: _____

FAST LASHES

You'll need someone's help to count this one: How many times can you wink in five seconds?

First Attempt: _____

My Amazing World Record: _____

How much does your count change when you wink with just your left eye, with just your right eye, and switching back and forth between the two?

99,98,97,
96,95,94,93, 92...

HINT: 99 COMES FIRST

Count backward from 100 out loud. How far did you get in five seconds?

First Attempt: _____

My Amazing World Record: _____

KAN YOU KANGAROO?

How many times can you hop up and down in five seconds? (Both feet: Don't cheat!)

First Attempt: _____

My Amazing World Record: _____

BURST OF APPLAUSE

How many times can you clap in five seconds?

First Attempt: _____

My Amazing World Record: _____

SUPER FAST THUMB

Get a clickable ball-point pen. How many times can you click it in and out in five seconds?

First Attempt: _____

My Amazing World Record: _____

Amazing Fact

The average American will live more than two billion seconds. If you live to be 100 (good luck!), how many seconds will that be?

HOT SEAT

How many times can you sit down and stand up in the same chair in five seconds?

First Attempt: _____

My Amazing World Record: _____

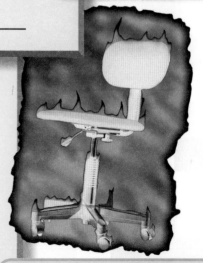

(ANSWER: 3,153,600,000)

10-SECOND DASHES

The world's fastest runners can sprint the length of a football field in 10 seconds. See how you do in these 10-second challenges.

FLYING FEAT!

In 10 seconds, make the best paper airplane you can. How far can it fly? Record your best distance.

First Attempt: _____

My Amazing World Record: _____

TENNIS TOSS

You'll need a bunch of tennis balls for this: Put a bucket 10 feet away, and see how many balls you can toss into the bucket in 10 seconds. Then move it 15 feet away and try again!

First Attempt: _____

My Amazing World Record: _____

Amazing Fact

The first person to run 100 meters in less than 10 seconds was Jim Hines. The U.S. sprinter won gold in the 1968 Olympics with a time of 9.95 seconds.

BEAT THE BOLT

In 2009, Usain Bolt of Jamaica set the 100-meter world record: 9.58 seconds. How far can you run in 10 seconds? Tip: Use a measuring tape for this one!

First Attempt: _____

My Amazing World Record: _____

MOTORMOUTH

How high can you count out loud in 10 seconds using only odd numbers?

First Attempt: _____

My Amazing World Record: _____

How high can you count using only even numbers?

First Attempt: _____

My Amazing World Record: _____

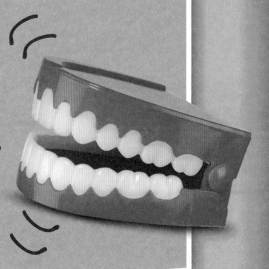

CRUNCH TIME!

How many sit-ups can you pull off in 10 seconds?

First Attempt: _____

My Amazing World Record: _____

Now see how many push-ups you can do in that time!

First Attempt: _____

My Amazing World Record: _____

Mega-Challenge: How many jumping jacks can you do in 10 seconds?

First Attempt: _____

My Amazing World Record: _____

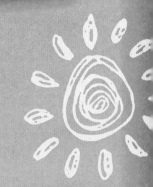

20-second silliness!

What is 20 seconds? It's one-third of a minute, or about five-thousandths of an hour. Bet you don't think you can get much done in that amount of time. We bet you can!

SUPER SOCK-A-THON

How many socks can you put on one foot in 20 seconds?

First Attempt: _____

**My Amazing
World Record:** _____

QUARTER TURNS

How many quarters can you keep spinning like tops in 20 seconds? They must stay spinning to count.

First Attempt: _____

**My Amazing
World Record:** _____

TWIST YOUR TONGUE

In 20 seconds, how many times can you say, "Silly Sally slurps soda slowly"?

First Attempt: _____

**My Amazing
World Record:** _____

NOT-SO-SHORT SNORT

How many times can you snort like a pig in 20 seconds?

First Attempt: _____

**My Amazing
World Record:** _____

Honk like a goose?

First Attempt: _____

**My Amazing
World Record:** _____

Crow like a rooster? (Feel silly yet?)

First Attempt: _____

**My Amazing
World Record:** _____

WORK YOUR WHISTLER!

See if you can whistle nonstop for 20 seconds...all in one breath! How many tries did it take you to do it?

First Attempt: _____

**My Amazing
World Record:** _____

45 Seconds to Greatness

In a minute, we'll get to what you can do in a minute. But first, let's make a pit stop on the clock. Is 45 seconds a long time? Or a short time? After you do these challenges, cast your vote!

PENNY PILES

How many pennies can you stack in 45 seconds...while blindfolded?

First Attempt: _____

**My Amazing
World Record:** _____

QUICK-CHANGE ARTIST

How many times can you take off your shirt and pants and put them back on again in 45 seconds?

First Attempt: _____

**My Amazing
World Record:** _____

FEEL THE BURN!

Find a staircase at least 10 stairs tall. How many times can you get up and down (be careful!) in 45 seconds?

First Attempt: _____

**My Amazing
World Record:** _____

JUST JUMPING

How many times can you jump rope in 45 seconds? If you trip on the rope, start your count again.

First Attempt: _____

**My Amazing
World Record:** _____

★ Record to Beat! ★

In 2006, 292 engineering students in Pune, India, successfully jumped rope simultaneously on the same rope, setting a Guinness World Record.

Got a Minute?

A minute has 60 seconds. You will need every single one to prove your awesomeness. For all of these challenges it takes just a minute...to win it!

Mississippi

BE PEN-TASTIC!

How many times in 60 seconds can you write the word "Mississippi"?

First Attempt: _____

**My Amazing
World Record:** _____

To give your mouth a workout, too, see how many times you can say it in a minute!

First Attempt: _____

**My Amazing
World Record:** _____

52-CARD SHUFFLE

Take a deck of cards, dump them onto the floor faceup, and spread them around. In 60 seconds, how many can you put back in order? (Remember to start with all the aces, then all the 2s, 3s, 4s...)

First Attempt: _____

**My Amazing
World Record:** _____

WALL BALL

Grab a ball…and a wall. Stand five feet away and bounce the ball against the wall, catching it before it hits the ground. How many times can you bounce and catch in 60 seconds?

First Attempt: _____

**My Amazing
World Record:** _____

1-2-3-4-5…WHEW!

How many of these ||||| can you write in one minute? Count the groups of five, not the individual lines.

First Attempt: _____

**My Amazing
World Record:** _____

AS EASY AS Z-Y-X!

Can you recite the alphabet backward in 60 seconds? Try doing it without looking at the letters!

First Attempt: _____

**My Amazing
World Record:** _____

Amazing Fact

Soldiers in the American Revolution were known as "minutemen." It was said they could dress to be ready to join a battle…in just a minute!

Z Y X W V U T S R Q P O N
M L K J I H G F E D C B A

5-Minute Marathons

After doing things in 5, 10, or 20 seconds, the challenges on this page will seem like they take a *realllly* long time! But sometimes the hardest things take the most time!

DOMINO DROP

How many dominoes can you line up in five minutes? When your time is up, send them toppling! Only the dominoes that fell count toward your record!

First Attempt: _____

My Amazing World Record: _____

FILL 'ER UP

You need a large drinking glass and a tablespoon. Put the glass at least 20 feet away from a sink or a hose. How much of the glass can you fill in five minutes using only the spoon to carry water?

First Attempt: _____

My Amazing World Record: _____

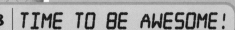

A REAL RUN-ON

Get a pencil and paper. Ready? Now write the longest sentence you can in five minutes. The sentence has to make sense (mostly!). Use lots of commas and dashes to keep it going. Measure how you did by counting the words.

First Attempt: _____

**My Amazing
World Record:** _____

A RUNNING READ-ON

Prefer reading to writing? Get a favorite book. How much of it can you read out loud in five minutes? Measure by counting how many book lines you read. Remember to breathe!

First Attempt: _____

**My Amazing
World Record:** _____

ROUND AND ROUND

How many times can you run around the outside of your house or building in five minutes?

First Attempt: _____

**My Amazing
World Record:** _____

Take a breather…and then set the record for backward running!

First Attempt: _____

**My Amazing
World Record:** _____

★ **Record
to Beat!** ★

Achim Aretz of Germany holds the world record for fastest marathon run…backward! He ran (or did he "nar"?) his 26.2 miles in 3 hours, 42 minutes in 2010.

HOW LONG CAN YOU...

Many world records are set for endurance—people doing the same thing for a *lonnnng* time. For each of these challenges, see how long you can do it…and then see if you can do better the next time! (Some of these could take days…)

HANG IN THERE

Remember, for these challenges, there is no time limit. In fact, the longer the better! Record how long you can…

	First Attempt	**My Amazing World Record**
Stare without blinking	_____	_____
Stand on one foot	_____	_____
Hold a push-up position	_____	_____
Hold an orange straight out in front of you	_____	_____
Balance a balloon on your head	_____	_____
Hold your breath	_____	_____
Bounce a ball	_____	_____
Maintain a big smile	_____	_____
Keep your room clean	_____	_____

(Nah, just kidding…no one can do that for long!)

FLYING FEATHERS!

For this challenge, you need a feather. Pick one that's fluffy and light, not stiff with a hard point. Now see how long you can keep it floating above your head using only your breath to keep it up there. Huff and puff and don't let it fall!

First Attempt: _____

My Amazing World Record: _____

SUPER ENDURANCE CHALLENGES!

Record how long you can…

	First Attempt	My Amazing World Record
Do everything with your opposite hand		
Go without using the word "like"		
Wear a shirt backward before someone notices		
Not eat any candy		
Not wear the color blue		
Walk backward everywhere		
Start every sentence with "Yo,…"		
Speak with an English accent		

(If you're English, try speaking with a French accent!)

Paper Pastimes

Paper performers: Please procure pieces of paper…and patience. And perhaps a pen. (P.S.: Plain notebook paper will work perfectly.)

LINE 'EM UP!

How many times can you write your name on a piece of paper that is 5 x 7 inches? None of the names can touch or cross.

First Attempt: _____

**My Amazing
World Record:** _____

SECRET SEVEN

How many times can you fold one piece of paper in half?

First Attempt: _____

**My Amazing
World Record:** _____

CHAIN CHALLENGE

Using one piece of paper, make the longest paper chain you can. The narrower and shorter the strips of paper you cut, the longer your chain will be!

First Attempt: _____

**My Amazing
World Record:** _____

RIP IT UP!

Use a full sheet of notebook paper for this one. What is the longest strip of paper you can rip from the sheet? (Here's a hint…rip in a spiral.)

First Attempt: _____

My Amazing World Record: _____

Amazing Fact

See all those "p"s in the introduction? That's called alliteration. Many tongue twisters use alliteration. For example: **F***rantic* **F***rancis* **f***ries* **f***resh* **f***ranks.*

NEWS HAT?

Do you know how to make a hat out of newspaper? If not, ask Mom or Dad or look on the Internet. How fast can you fold one of your own?

First Attempt: _____

My Amazing World Record: _____

Once you are an expert, how fast can you fold it with your eyes closed?

First Attempt: _____

My Amazing World Record: _____

BONUS CHALLENGE:

How long can you make a sentence in which ALL the words start with the same letter? It must make sense!

First Attempt: _____

My Amazing World Record: _____

School Supplies

Your teacher gives you a list of stuff you need for school. You need that stuff to do your work. But that doesn't mean you can't have fun with it, too! Dig into your school supplies for the materials you need to master these challenges.

STICK WITH IT!

How many sticky notes can you stick to your face in 30 seconds? They have to stay on the whole time!

First Attempt: _____

**My Amazing
World Record:** _____

How many can you stick on one arm?

First Attempt: _____

**My Amazing
World Record:** _____

Super Challenge: How many can you stick on your body with no time limit? They have to stay stuck to count!

First Attempt: _____

**My Amazing
World Record:** _____

PENCIL PUSHERS

How fast can you spell "pencil"? Wait—there's a trick. You have to use several pencils to form the shapes of letters one at a time on a table!

First Attempt: _____

**My Amazing
World Record:** _____

LEANING TOWER OF CLIP-PISA

Paper clips are known for holding things together. But how many can you stack up to make a paper-clip tower without it falling over?

First Attempt: _____

**My Amazing
World Record:** _____

WRAP IT UP!

A tennis ball is pretty bouncy. Make it bouncier! How fast can you wrap 25 rubber bands around a tennis ball?

First Attempt: _____

**My Amazing
World Record:** _____

YOUR NAME IN METAL

Test your stapling abilities! How fast can you use a stapler to form letters that spell your name in a piece of paper?

First Attempt: _____

**My Amazing
World Record:** _____

TOYS GALORE

You'll need to gather some other props for setting these world marks. Record setters: to the toy box!

CEILING SCRAPERS

What is the tallest single-brick Lego tower you can build?

First Attempt: _____

**My Amazing
World Record:** _____

Then try for the longest wall you can build that is two bricks high.

First Attempt: _____

**My Amazing
World Record:** _____

POP GOES THE RECORD

Bubble time! Blow soap bubbles and see how long you can keep one from popping. It's easiest if you blow one at a time!

First Attempt: _____

**My Amazing
World Record:** _____

STUFFED WITH FRIENDS

How many stuffed animals can you stuff inside your shirt? How many more can you fit if someone helps?

First Attempt: _____

**My Amazing
World Record:** _____

MEGA-BOUNCE

You need a small super-bouncy ball and a mug.
Set the mug against a wall. Stand six feet away and
bounce the ball into the mug. How many tries does
it take to get the ball in?

First Attempt: _____

**My Amazing
World Record:** _____

Super Challenge: Use three balls and three mugs.
How many tries does it take to get one ball in each mug?

First Attempt: _____

**My Amazing
World Record:** _____

MINI-MARATHON

Find a small toy car and a long hallway. What is the longest
distance you can make the car roll (not fly!) in a single push?

First Attempt: _____

**My Amazing
World Record:** _____

Amazing Fact

*In 2008, artists and
designers at Hot Wheels
made a toy car worth
$140,000! The one-
of-a-kind car was
covered in diamonds.
The brake lights were
made of rubies!*

Silence and Sounds

Some world records are barely heard. Others are blasted from the rooftops! See which ones you're better at.

SHHHHHH!

How long can you go without making any noise at all…not even a cough? (No fair setting this record while you sleep!)

First Attempt: _____

My Amazing World Record: _____

OPERA TIME!

Stand next to a piano (though not one at a store; you might frighten the customers). Sing the lowest note you possibly can, and find that note on the piano. Then sing the highest note you can, and find it on the piano. How many white keys are in between your lowest and highest notes?

First Attempt: _____

My Amazing World Record: _____

HMMMMM

How long can you hum without taking a breath? Try it at different volumes for different results.

First Attempt: _____

My Amazing World Record: _____

BOOIINNNG!

Get a friend to help you with this. Have him sit down while turned away from you and close his eyes. Take off your shoes. How many times can you jump up and down before your friend hears you doing it?

First Attempt: _____

My Amazing World Record: _____

Amazing Fact

In 2013, fans at Arrowhead Stadium in Kansas City, Missouri, became the loudest ever in an outdoor stadium. Their cheers reached 137.5 decibels. A decibel is a unit that measures sound. To compare, a jet engine roars at 140 decibels!

OH, SNAP, PART 1

How far away can you get from a friend and snap your fingers loud enough for him to hear you?

First Attempt: _____

My Amazing World Record: _____

Body Art

For these challenges, your personal world record gets a bit more personal. See how you do when your own personal person is the place where you set the records!

DON'T PINCH

How many clothespins can you attach to one ear at one time? You can attach clothespins to other clothespins to do this challenge!

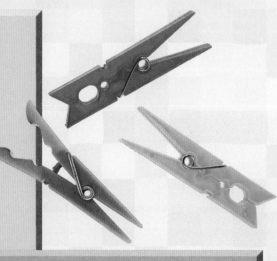

First Attempt: _____

**My Amazing
World Record:** _____

TIGHT FIT

What is the smallest T-shirt you can fit completely on your body? Kids small? Toddler sizes? Try to do it without ripping anything!

First Attempt: _____

**My Amazing
World Record:** _____

STRETTTTCH

How high up a wall can you reach? Stretch as far as you can. Then limber up and see if you can reach even higher!

First Attempt: _____

**My Amazing
World Record:** _____

TATTOO YOU!

How many temporary tattoos can you apply to one of your arms? They can't overlap!

First Attempt: _____

**My Amazing
World Record:** _____

HAT RACK

You might need help for this one. How many hats can you wear on your head at one time? You can ask a friend for help if the stack gets too high to reach.

First Attempt: _____

**My Amazing
World Record:** _____

HOUDINI!

While barefoot, have a friend tie your hands together with a scarf or a sock. Now see how fast you can pull on your socks and then pull on and tie your sneakers!

First Attempt: _____

**My Amazing
World Record:** _____

Amazing Fact

No baseball player could wear the giant hats that were built outside Angel Stadium in Anaheim, California. Most players wear about a size 7 hat. The massive domes at the ballpark are size 849½!

PENCIL POWER

Test your writing and drawing abilities with these artistic challenges. Don't worry; you won't be graded! No art expertise needed!

SHAPE UP OR SHIP OUT!

How fast can you draw all these shapes onto one yellow sticky note: square, rectangle, octagon, circle, oval, heart, triangle, pentagon, and diamond?

First Attempt: _____

**My Amazing
World Record:** _____

Amazing Fact

One famous shape is also one of the world's largest buildings. The Pentagon in Washington, D.C., has more than 17 miles of corridors!

GET THE POINT?

How long can you balance a pencil on one finger using just the point? See if you can do it longer using the eraser end.

First Attempt: _____

**My Amazing
World Record:** _____

REVERSE WRITE!

How fast can you write the entire alphabet…
with each letter upside down?

First Attempt: _____

**My Amazing
World Record:** _____

BLIND DOG

Look at a picture of a dog (or at a real dog if you have one handy!).
Now close your eyes and try to draw a picture of that dog in 60 seconds.
Show your drawing to a friend. Can they guess it is a dog?

First Attempt: _____

**Second
Attempt:** _____

Use a different dog and draw it in 30 seconds!

First Attempt: _____

**Second
Attempt:** _____

WRITERS' MARATHON

How many numbers can you write backward before
you make a mistake? Use a mirror to check your
work after each number!

First Attempt: _____

**My Amazing
World Record:** _____

CHOPSTICK CHALLENGE!

Are you a super picker-upper? Prove it! Using chopsticks, how many of each of these things can you pick up in one minute? *Zhù nî háoyùn!* (That means "good luck" in Chinese.)

First Attempt

My Amazing World Record

Little Things:

Grains of rice

Marbles

Pieces of string

Paper clips

Lego pieces

Tubes of lip balm

Safety pins

Cotton balls

Rings

Fingernail clippers

Small erasers

Pieces of raw spaghetti

Pennies/dimes

Thumbtacks

(Bonus: Try pulling them out of a bulletin board!)

Bigger Things:

Another pair of chopsticks

A baseball

An orange

A sneaker

A cell phone

A wet bar of soap

SUPER-DUPER CHALLENGE

Want to amaze your friends and family? Learn a new incredible skill—like being able to use chopsticks with either hand. It will take lots of practice. But once you learn it, you will find many ways to impress others. Once you are a chopstick master, see how many of these things you can do using one or two sets of sticks!

❏ Put on your socks.

❏ Tie your shoe. If you can't make a bow, aim for a simple knot.

❏ Play a card game in which you must use the chopsticks to draw and discard.

❏ Read a book and use the chopsticks to hold it and turn the pages.

❏ Make your bed!

❏ Eat your breakfast, lunch, and dinner!

What other things can you think of?

_____

_____

Amazing Fact

People in China have been using chopsticks for more than 3,000 years. By 500 A.D., chopsticks had spread to other Asian countries.

READY, SET, RACE!

Time to find out who is the fastest...sort of. These races challenge more than just your feet! It's best if one of your friends sits out to time and judge the races. Take turns being the timer!

RACE LIKE AN ANIMAL!

In this race, get into a frog position and get hopping! First person to hop 15 yards is the winner! Who was the fastest frog? What was his time?

Fastest Frog:_____ **Time:**_____

My Time: _____

Now get down on a clean floor and slither like a snake! Who can get to the finish line first without using hands or arms to help move forward?

Swiftest Snake: _____ **Time:**_____

My Time: _____

Put four on the floor and race like a greyhound! You must run on all fours—no jumping allowed! Who was top dog?

Top Dog: _____ **Time:**_____

My Time: _____

A CLASSIC!

The wheelbarrow race has been around for years. Find a flat space outside, measure out 50 feet, and get racing! How fast was the winning wheelbarrow?

The Winner: _____ **Time:** _____

My Time: _____

Make the race longer! At the 50-foot marker, switch places and head back to the start. How fast was the winning team?

Winning Team: _____ **Time:** _____

My Time: _____

CHINNY-CHIN-CHIN

For this race, each participant needs to hold a ball under his chin while running (tennis balls and baseballs work well). First person to run 25 yards without dropping his ball wins!

The Winner: _____

My Time: _____

INFLATE-A-THON

Grab a bag of balloons, and give three empty balloons to each friend. Blow up one balloon to use as a "model balloon." Then get blowing! Which friend can blow up their three balloons to be the same size as the model the fastest?

The Winner: _____ **Time:** _____

My Time: _____

Amazing Fact

A man knitted a 12-foot-long scarf. No big deal, right? Well, he did it while running a marathon in Kansas City, Missouri, in 2013!

Crazy Calisthenics

Ready for a workout? Take on these challenges and set a stack of new amazing world records!

OVER AND OVER AND OVER...

Which friend in your group can do the most somersaults in a row? Do this challenge one at a time or as a group. How many somersaults did the super somersaulter do? (Say that five times fast!)

The Winner: _____ **How Many:** _____

My Amazing World Record: _____

MONKEYING AROUND

Head to a playground that has monkey bars. Have each person hang from a bar for as long as he can. Who's the top banana? How long was he hanging?

The Winner: _____ **Time:** _____

My Amazing World Record: _____

SIT-UP SURPRISE!

Gather a group of your best athletes—and see who can do the most sit-ups in 90 seconds!

The Winner: _____ **How Many:** _____

**My Amazing
World Record:** _____

Who can do sit-ups for the longest time without stopping?

The Winner: _____ **How Many:** _____

**My Amazing
World Record:** _____

HIGH-SPEED JUMPING JACKS

Jumping jacks are most fun when done fast. They can also be exhausting! Gather your best friends and see who can do the most in one minute.

The Winner: _____ **How Many:** _____

**My Amazing
World Record:** _____

GROUP PLANK!

Do you know the starting push-up position? Straight back, straight arms, knees off the ground. Get a big group together and see who can hold that position the longest!

The Winner: _____ **Time:** _____

**My Amazing
World Record:** _____

off-the-Wall Wardrobes

Time to hit the closet for the gear you need to face these challenges. No fashion sense needed—just a sense of adventure and fun! (Though fast fingers might help, too!)

READY, SET, KNOT!

Get some friends together and divide into pairs. Now see which pair can tie all their shoes the fastest. Here's the trick—you each can use only one hand. But you can work together to tie each shoe!

The Winners: _____ **Time:** _____

My Amazing World Record: _____

SHIRT RELAY

Find a really big T-shirt. Now see how fast you can relay-wear it! What's your best time for everyone in the group to put it on and take it off in turn?

First Attempt: _____

Our Amazing World Record: _____

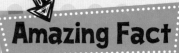

Amazing Fact

In 2010, more than 2,000 Boy Scouts teamed up to tie knots in a rope...all at once! In five minutes, they created a single strand that measured 9,774 feet!

A SLEEVE-A-PEDE

This one needs long-sleeved shirts and many friends. How long a line can you make with people grabbing their partners' arms inside one another's sleeves? Sort of like a human chain, but all covered in shirts!

First Attempt: _____

**Our Amazing
World Record:** _____

BUTTON-UP

You will need a button-down shirt for each challenger. Unbutton the shirts, blindfold each person, and then get buttoning! Who buttoned his shirt perfectly (all buttons in the correct holes) the fastest?

The Winner: _____ **Time:** _____

**My Amazing
World Record:** _____

SIZE

XXXXL

REALLY BIG SHIRT

Find the most enormous quadruple-XL T-shirt you can. Ask your local football team. Or try a "big and tall" men's store. Then see how many of your friends can get inside it at once.

First Attempt: _____

**Our Amazing
World Record:** _____

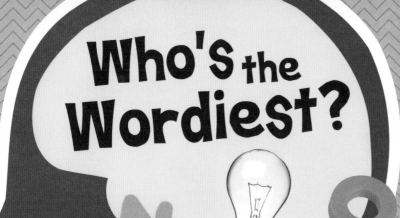

Who's the Wordiest?

Many brains make for some pretty awesome work! For these challenges, work with or compete against your buddies to see who has the fastest word brain!

Amazing Fact

Here are some of the most recent popular boys' names given to babies born around the world.

U.S.A.: *Jackson*
England: *Harry*
France: *Nathan*
Japan: *Haruto*
Russia: *Danil*
Turkey: *Berat*

HIDDEN WORDS

How many words can your group make using only the letters from the words AMAZING ME?

First Attempt: _____

**Our Amazing
World Record:** _____

Now use the letters from BATRACHOPHAGOUS. Bonus points if you can guess what it means.

First Attempt: _____

**Our Amazing
World Record:** _____

What were the longest words you came up with for both challenges?

First Attempt: _____

**Our Amazing
World Record:** _____

READY TO WRITE?

For these challenges, the goal is to write as many words on a piece of paper as possible that fit the challenge. Put one minute on the clock for each challenge. Spelling counts! Record who wins each event!

Write as many two-letter words as you can in one minute. (Hey, we just gave you two right there! Yikes! There's another one!)

Winner: _____ **How Many Words:**_____

Let's make it harder...how many three-letter words can you scribble in one minute?

Winner: _____ **How Many Words:**_____

Now make it seven-letter words! Awesome!

Winner: _____ **How Many Words:**_____

How many two-syllable verbs? Go!

Winner: _____ **How Many Words:**_____

CHILL BILL AND TALL PAUL

How many words can you think of that rhyme with your name?

Number of Words: _____

Compete to see whose name is the rhymiest. Whose name had the most rhymes? You can also work together to come up with the longest list for all your names.

Who Is Rhymiest: _____

My Amazing World Record: _____

BUILD IT UP!

Start with any letter, then take turns adding one letter at a time. What's the longest word you can make that way? Keep trying...there are some great words out there!

First Attempt: _____

Our Amazing World Record: _____

ARE YOU SUPER SCAVENGERS?

Break into two teams and decide if you want to scavenge inside or outside. Set a timer for 15 minutes for the indoor list and 45 minutes for the outdoor list. Keep the list somewhere everyone can refer to it. The team that finds the most objects in that time is the winner. Scavengers can either gather the objects or use a digital camera or phone camera to take a photo of each thing.

OUTSIDE THE HOUSE

	Team 1	Team 2
Four different things that come from trees	☐	☐
Three pieces of litter	☐	☐
Two different types of grass	☐	☐
Three rocks of different colors	☐	☐
A living insect (be careful not to hurt it and be sure to let it go when the hunt is over)	☐	☐
Two red, yellow, or white objects of any kind that are not human-made	☐	☐
A seed	☐	☐
A Y-shaped stick	☐	☐
A feather	☐	☐
Something smooth	☐	☐
Something pointy	☐	☐

Total objects scavenged: _____ _____

INSIDE THE HOUSE

	Team 1	Team 2
An object with a name that starts with "O"	☐	☐
Something that writes in a color other than blue or black	☐	☐
An item of clothing at least three years old	☐	☐
Something with your picture on or in it	☐	☐
A drinking glass with words on it	☐	☐
Five socks that do not match	☐	☐
A book that is at least 150 pages long	☐	☐
A picture of food you would eat at breakfast	☐	☐
Any image of an animal other than a dog or cat	☐	☐
A pot holder	☐	☐
A spoon big enough to hold a baseball	☐	☐
A spice with a name that starts with the letter "T"	☐	☐
Four things that you use to clean up	☐	☐

Total objects scavenged: _____   _____

The next time you have a group of friends together, try this challenge again! Were you able to beat your total?

Ridiculous Relays

Keep time to see which team is the fastest!

For each of these relays, measure and mark a course that is about 15 yards from start to finish. Split your friends into even-numbered teams. Half the racers stand at the start line and half stand at the 15-yard finish line. Each racer must do the task given, then tag the next racer, who then returns to where the first racer came from (and tags the next racer).

DON'T EAT THE GAME PIECES!

You need a spoon for each racer and some small candies. Each racer must run with the candy in his spoon to the next racer and transfer the candy to the next person's spoon. If the candy is dropped at any time, the racer must go back to the start!

Winning Team: _____ **Time:** _____

Second Place: _____ **Time:** _____

PIGGYBACK

Piggyback time: Hop on for a ride to the 15-yard mark. Then switch positions and race back. Make sure all racers pair up according to size!

Winning Team: _____ **Time:** _____

Second Place: _____ **Time:** _____

> ★ **Record to Beat!** ★
>
> In 2012, four men from Jamaica set the 4x100-meter world record: 36.84 seconds. They were competing at the Olympic Games in London.

ORANGE YOU GLAD YOU BRUSHED?

Get up close and personal with your best buddies. For this relay, you must run with an orange under your chin. To tag your partner, you must pass the orange to him without using your hands!

Winning Team: _____ **Time:** _____

Second Place: _____ **Time:** _____

WATCH THE BALLOON!

Use large balloons for this relay. Each racer must keep a balloon in the air while running to the next racer. If the balloon touches the ground, go back to the start!

Winning Team: _____ **Time:** _____

Second Place: _____ **Time:** _____

ON AND OFF...AND ON

You need a hat, a big jacket, and some large shoes. The first person puts everything on and runs to the next person and takes those clothes off. The second person then puts on the same hat, jacket, and shoes. And so on...first team to have everyone dress and undress wins!

Winning Team: _____ **Time:** _____

Second Place: _____ **Time:** _____

For an extra challenge, add sweatpants. For an even bigger challenge, make the course 30 yards!

ONE-ON-ONE COMPETITIONS

For all of these challenges, two people compete against each other at once. If you have enough people, set up a play-off system and see who emerges as the champion!

BOOK IT!

Who can make the tallest tower of stacked books in 30 seconds? There is a twist…the books must be standing up, not lying flat!

Super Stacker: _____ **How Many:** _____

My Amazing World Record: _____

GOT BAT?

Who can balance a baseball bat on his finger for the longest?

The Winner: _____ **Time:** _____

My Amazing World Record: _____

Now see who can walk the farthest while doing just that!

The Winner: _____ **Time:** _____

My Amazing World Record: _____

FORE! (OR MORE!)

Get a bunch of golf balls (at least 12). Who can hold the most in one hand (stacking them is okay)?

The Winner: _____ **How Many:** _____

My Amazing World Record: _____

THUMBTHING FUN!

Prepare for a war! Grab your opponent's hand and see who wins two out of three thumb wars while both of you are blindfolded!

The Winner: _____

FACE-TO-FACE

This is a challenge of balance and comedy. Stand on one foot face-to-face with your opponent, two feet apart. Now make silly faces. No touching! Whoever puts his foot down first is the loser! Who can stand that way the longest?

The Winner: _____

Time: _____

Challenge Your Class!

The other group games were for random sets of kids. These are for one class at a time. Ask your teacher to help organize these and see what sort of records you set...together!

OH, SNAP, PART II

How many group snaps can your class make in a row? They have to be completely simultaneous, which means at the exact same moment. They need to sound like one giant snap!

First Attempt: _____

Our Amazing World Record: _____

Amazing Fact

A man in Morocco named Brahim Takioulla has the longest foot in the world. It's literally a foot (and three inches) long!

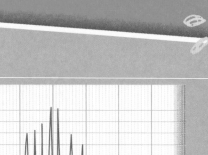

EARTHQUAKE!

How many times can you all jump together? Everyone has to be off the ground at once! Your teacher should keep watch and count.

First Attempt: _____

Our Amazing World Record: _____

TOGETHERNESS

See how long you can go at recess with your entire class holding hands.
No matter where you go and no matter whose nose itches, hold on!
Time yourselves and see if you can improve from day to day!

First Attempt: _____

**Our Amazing
World Record:** _____

SHOE SCRAMBLE

Put all your shoes into a large box. Put the box 25
yards away. Then race to see how long it takes all
the kids in your class to get all their shoes back on
and race back to the start. All laces must be tied!

First Attempt: _____

**Our Amazing
World Record:** _____

TALK-A-THON

Line up and see how fast your entire class can say the alphabet with each person saying
one letter at a time. Then see how high you can count—one at a time—in one minute.

Alphabet: _____   **Counting:** _____

**Our Amazing
World Record:** _____   **Our Amazing
World Record:** _____

Power in Pairs!

Three's a crowd, but two's a team! Get your best pal and set a stack of personal world records together. How many times can you do each of these activities? Not all at once, though that would be fun to try, too!

HOW MANY TIMES CAN YOU.....

	First Attempt	Our Amazing World Record
Toss a water balloon back and forth without dropping it?		
From 6 feet away	_____	_____
From 10 feet away	_____	_____
From 20 feet away	_____	_____
Toss a raw egg back and forth? Game is over when it breaks!		
From 4 feet away	_____	_____
From 8 feet away	_____	_____
From 12 feet away	_____	_____
Throw a Frisbee back and forth (catching it each time)?		
From 20 feet away	_____	_____
From 30 feet away	_____	_____
From 40 feet away	_____	_____
Kick a ball back and forth without missing? One kick each time!		
From 10 feet away	_____	_____
From 20 feet away	_____	_____
From 30 feet away	_____	_____

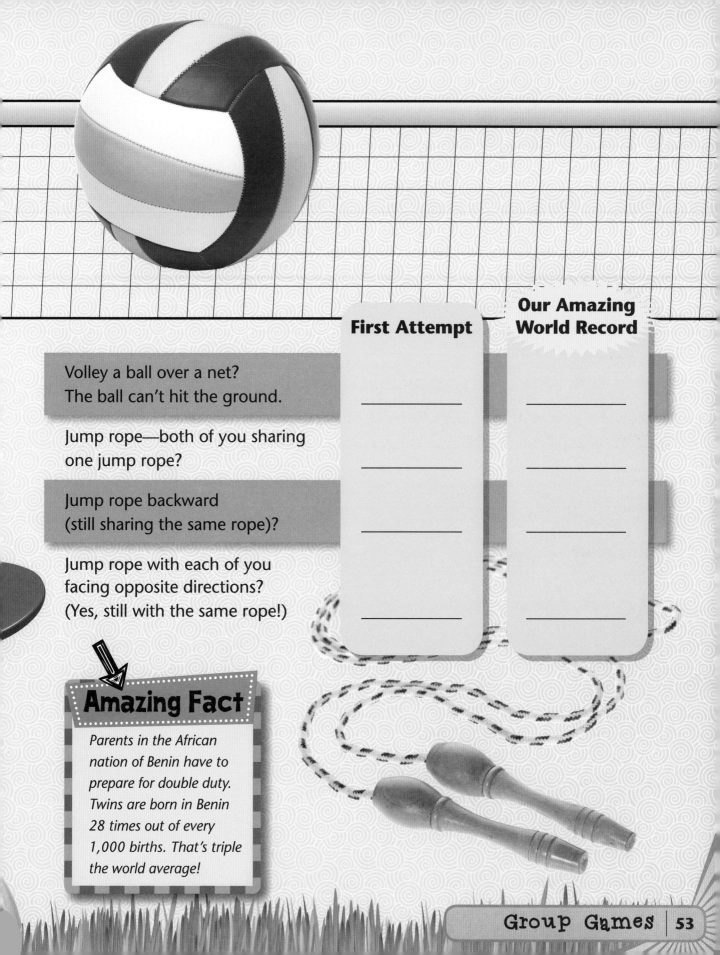

	First Attempt	**Our Amazing World Record**
Volley a ball over a net? The ball can't hit the ground.	_____	_____
Jump rope—both of you sharing one jump rope?	_____	_____
Jump rope backward (still sharing the same rope)?	_____	_____
Jump rope with each of you facing opposite directions? (Yes, still with the same rope!)	_____	_____

Amazing Fact

Parents in the African nation of Benin have to prepare for double duty. Twins are born in Benin 28 times out of every 1,000 births. That's triple the world average!

Fantastic Gymnastics

Olympic gymnasts have to be flexible, strong, and brave. For these active activities, you just have to do your best…and that might be enough to set a record!

HAND WALKER

Get help from a friend. Have him hold your legs while you do a handstand. Then see how far you can "walk" before your arms get too tired to continue.

First Attempt: _____

My Amazing World Record: _____

Super Challenge: How far can you handstand-walk *without* your friend holding your legs?

First Attempt: _____

My Amazing World Record: _____

Amazing Fact

The man with the most Olympic gymnastics medals is Nikolay Andrianov of the Soviet Union. He won 15 medals, including seven golds, while competing from 1972 to 1980.

BALANCE CURB

Find a long, low curb and make like a gymnast. How far can you walk this narrow balance beam without toppling?

First Attempt: _____

My Amazing World Record: _____

For more of a challenge, mark out a distance and see how fast you can walk it.

HOOP DIVE

Have a friend hold a Hula-Hoop so that it is straight up and down about a foot above the ground. How many times can you jump back and forth through it in a minute?

First Attempt: _____

**My Amazing
World Record:** _____

Super Challenge: Now have him hold the hoop two or three feet off the ground!

First Attempt: _____

**My Amazing
World Record:** _____

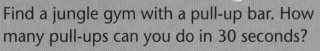

BE A TREE!

Stand up straight and lift one foot and place it just above your other leg's knee. How long can you stay balanced in this position before you have to put your foot down?

First Attempt: _____

**My Amazing
World Record:** _____

RAISING THE BAR

Find a jungle gym with a pull-up bar. How many pull-ups can you do in 30 seconds?

First Attempt: _____

**My Amazing
World Record:** _____

Then set your own record for most in a row until you have to let go!

First Attempt: _____

**My Amazing
World Record:** _____

RUN, LEAP, THROW

Track and field is one of the biggest parts of the Olympic Games. The track is obvious: You run on it. The field is all the other stuff: jumping, throwing, and vaulting! Check out these T&F events and see if you get the gold!

THE SOARING SOCK

Instead of the hammer throw, it's the sock toss! Stuff your biggest sock with five other socks. Twirl and fling! How far can you launch it? (Too far for your measuring tape? See page 7 for how to make a measuring string.)

First Attempt: _____

My Amazing World Record: _____

STAND AND LEAP

Olympic long jumpers get a running start. In this one, you don't! Put your feet together and jump as far as you can. Measure from where your heels land. How far did you jump?

First Attempt: _____

My Amazing World Record: _____

THE 25-YARD HSAD!*

*That's "dash" backward…and that's what you have to do. How fast can you run 25 yards…backward?

First Attempt: _____

**My Amazing
World Record:** _____

SPEAR THE SPOT

Olympic athletes throw the spear-like javelin. Take a straight stick about three feet long and see if you can hit a one-foot target from 10 feet away…then back up. From how far away can you throw it on target?

First Attempt: _____

**My Amazing
World Record:** _____

HOW LOW WILL YOU GO?

Instead of the high jump, we'll do the low crawl. Have friends hold a stick or pole. Crawl under it. How low can the bar be to the ground before you can't make it under?

First Attempt: _____

**My Amazing
World Record:** _____

Amazing Fact

American Ray Ewry won four straight Olympic gold medals in an odd event: the standing long jump. No run-up… just jump as far as you can. His best was 11 feet, 4 inches.

pools Rule!

Splish-splash, it's time to set some records. Head to the pool with a parent and try your best at these watery challenges. For many of these, it would be helpful to have a parent or friend keeping time!

WET WARDROBE

Grab a T-shirt, shorts, and a pair of socks and throw them into the shallow end of the pool. Now get in the pool and start timing. How long does it take to get dressed and out of the pool?

First Attempt: _____

My Amazing World Record: _____

Not challenging enough? Add a sweatshirt and jeans to your wet wardrobe!

First Attempt: _____

My Amazing World Record: _____

SPLASH SPRINT

How fast can you get across the pool? No, wait…not swimming. You have to run! (You have to do this one in the shallow end of the pool.)

First Attempt: _____

My Amazing World Record: _____

DIVE FOR FIVE (CENTS)

Have a friend or parent drop five pennies into the pool. How quickly can you get them all out of the water? You can remove only one at a time.

First Attempt: _____

**My Amazing
World Record:** _____

TRY IT WITH FRIENDS!

Toss five pennies, quarters, nickels, and dimes into the pool. After three minutes, stop the game and add up everyone's change. Who collected the most money?

Richest Friend: _____

My Grand Total: _____

POOL BALL

How fast can you get a balloon across the pool without touching it? Time to use your imagination!

First Attempt: _____

**My Amazing
World Record:** _____

Try the same thing with a Ping-Pong ball!

First Attempt: _____

**My Amazing
World Record:** _____

NOT A DROP!

Put on an old baseball cap. How fast can you swim (not walk) back and forth across the pool four times while keeping that hat completely dry? Watch out for splashes!

First Attempt: _____

**My Amazing
World Record:** _____

Break Out Your Bike!

You'll need a bike and your bike helmet for these challenges. You might also want to have some strength, balance, and courage handy, too!

FROZEN!

How long can you hold your bike in one place... with both feet on the pedals? Stop the timer when one of your feet touches the ground.

First Attempt: _____

**My Amazing
World Record:** _____

CIRCLE STOP!

Draw a small chalk circle on the ground (about three inches across). Pedal up to the circle and see how close you can come to stopping your front tire right on top of it. Measure how close you got.

First Attempt: _____

**My Amazing
World Record:** _____

ROLLER... COASTER

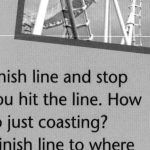

Mark out two lines on the ground 20 yards apart (start and finish lines).
Pedal toward the finish line and stop pedaling right as you hit the line. How far can you then go just coasting? Measure from the finish line to where you put your foot down.

First Attempt: _____

**My Amazing
World Record:** _____

SUPER-DUPER CYCLE CHALLENGE: WONDERFUL WEAVING

How much control do you have over your bike? Head to an empty parking lot, and let's get rolling! Set up eight cones in a line with about 10 feet between each cone. How fast can you weave through all the cones without knocking any over? Don't have cones? Use empty two-liter soda bottles!

First Attempt: _____

**My Amazing
World Record:** _____

Want a bigger challenge? Place the cones eight feet apart!

First Attempt: _____

**My Amazing
World Record:** _____

For experts only! Place the cones five feet apart.
Were you able to finish the course? How long did it take?

First Attempt: _____

**My Amazing
World Record:** _____

Now it's time to go slooooow. Place the cones six feet apart and weave through them as slowly as possible without putting your feet down or knocking over cones. Remember, you want to take as LONG as possible.

First Attempt: _____

**My Amazing
World Record:** _____

Amazing Fact

In 2012, English rider Mike Hall finished a bike ride. No big deal, right? Oh, did we mention he had just set a record for riding AROUND THE WORLD? It took him only 92 days. Wow!

SPORTS MANIA!

Cool word: "smorgasbord!" That means a mess of different foods, like a buffet. These challenges are a smorgasbord of sports!

LOOK, MA! NO HANDS!

The harder your noggin, the better for this challenge. How long can you keep a soccer ball in the air just using your head?

First Attempt: _____

My Amazing World Record: _____

Too tough? Try using your legs and feet to keep the soccer ball airborne!

GAZILLION-DRIBBLE

How long can you dribble a basketball without stopping, using your non-dominant hand (that's the hand you don't use to write)?

First Attempt: _____

My Amazing World Record: _____

OH, SHOOT!

How many baskets can you shoot in five minutes using only ONE hand to throw the basketball?

First Attempt: _____

My Amazing World Record: _____

WHAT A RACQUET!

Stand 15 feet away from a wall. How many times in a row can you hit a tennis ball against the wall with the racquet without missing? The ball must bounce once each time.

First Attempt: _____

My Amazing World Record: _____

Put a tennis ball on a tennis racquet. How many times can you run around a tennis court without the ball falling off?

First Attempt: _____

My Amazing World Record: _____

Next, try running while bouncing the ball on the racquet.

First Attempt: _____

My Amazing World Record: _____

Super Challenge: Think you are a ball-balancing expert? Put the ball on the rim or handle of the racquet, not the strings! How long can you keep the ball on the racquet?

First Attempt: _____

My Amazing World Record: _____

★ Record to Beat! ★

Free throws are basketball's easiest shots. But even the pros miss some. The NBA record for most free throws made in a row without a miss was set by Micheal Williams in 1993. The Minnesota Timberwolves guard made 97 straight! What's your record?

WINTER WONDERS

The Winter Olympics include sports that need snow or ice. These challenges also demand some winter weather. Grab your hat, coat, boots, and mittens and head out into the cold!

SUPER SWOOSH!

Head for the hills with your sled or snow tube! Always start from the same place. What is the longest ride you can take down the hill without stopping?

First Attempt: _____

My Amazing World Record: _____

Amazing Fact

The Winter Olympics medal king is Ole Einar Bjoerndalen. A biathlete from Norway, he won eight golds, four silvers, and a bronze. He picked up his latest two gold medals at Sochi in 2014.

Race a friend or two! Set up a finish line at the bottom of the hill. Who wins the most sled races out of 10?

First Attempt: _____

My Amazing World Record: _____

AMAZING ANGELS

You need a nice field of snow for this one (and gloves and a hat, probably!). In 30 seconds, how many complete snow angels can you make?

First Attempt: _____

My Amazing World Record: _____

ICE DARTS

Find some icicles and make a circular target on your lawn (about two feet across). Stand at least 30 feet away. How many bull's-eyes can you get out of five icicle throws?

First Attempt: _____

My Amazing World Record: _____

SNOWMAN?
SNOW MONSTER!

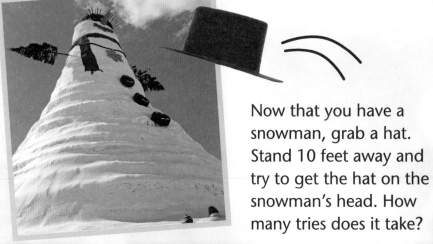

What is tallest snowman you can build? Can you get one over seven feet? You might need help from adults, but you can show them what to do. They're so clumsy!

Now that you have a snowman, grab a hat. Stand 10 feet away and try to get the hat on the snowman's head. How many tries does it take?

First Attempt: _____

My Amazing World Record: _____

First Attempt: _____

My Amazing World Record: _____

FROZEN FURY!

How many snowballs can you make in two minutes? Each has to be at least as big as a tennis ball.

First Attempt: _____

My Amazing World Record: _____

Race with a friend for two minutes to see who is the champion snowball maker!

First Attempt: _____

My Amazing World Record: _____

Super Challenge: What is the biggest snowball you can make? No rules here—you can roll it or pack snow onto it with your hands. Measure how big it is around.

First Attempt: _____

My Amazing World Record: _____

Throw for It!

Time to limber up and take a few flings. Let's see how you do with these throwing challenges. Are you better at being on target or throwing for distance?

PART 1: TARGET PRACTICE

Make a target out of cardboard, set it up, and stand about 15 feet away. How many bull's-eyes can you hit in one minute by throwing these things at the target? Have a friend keep time and stand safely nearby to count. They don't have to stick...just hit!

	First Attempt	My Amazing World Record
Pennies	_____	_____
Jelly beans	_____	_____
Pencils	_____	_____
Ping-Pong balls	_____	_____
Lego bricks	_____	_____
Paper clips	_____	_____
Tennis balls	_____	_____
Plastic forks	_____	_____
Wads of paper towels (dry)	_____	_____
Wads of paper towels (wet)	_____	_____

PART 2: CHUCK IT!

Clear some space! Find a field or a big playground and let fly! What's the best distance you can throw each of these items?

	First Attempt	My Amazing World Record
Football	_____	_____
Tennis ball	_____	_____
Wet sponge	_____	_____
Dry sponge	_____	_____
Paper airplane	_____	_____
Baseball cap	_____	_____
Sneaker	_____	_____
Marshmallow	_____	_____
Beach ball	_____	_____
Rubber duck	_____	_____
Frisbee	_____	_____
Playing card	_____	_____

Krazy Kitchen!

Time to have fun in the kitchen… and we don't mean doing dishes! Check with your folks before you start rummaging around the kitchen. Then see how you do with these challenges.

SPICE AS NICE

Get out all your family's jars of spices. Make sure you can read the labels. How fast can you line them up in alphabetical order?

First Attempt: _____

My Amazing World Record: _____

STACK 'EM UP!

You need 15 plastic cups about the same size. How quickly can you form a 5-4-3-2-1 pyramid with them?

First Attempt: _____

My Amazing World Record: _____

Now try this challenge with only one hand. What is your best time?

First Attempt: _____

My Amazing World Record: _____

Amazing Fact

The most expensive spice in the world is saffron. Used in Indian dishes, it can sell for as much as $5,000 per pound!

AN A-PEEL-ING CHALLENGE

What's the longest unbroken apple peel you can make? Be careful, as peelers are sharp. If you haven't peeled an apple before, ask a parent to show you the technique. Best part about this challenge? Every time you try, you get an apple to eat!

First Attempt: _____

**My Amazing
World Record:** _____

BLIND TREASURE HUNT

Take all the spoons you have in the house and put them in a small box (a shoe box works well). Then have someone add one fork to the box. While blindfolded, how long does it take you to find the fork?

First Attempt: _____

**My Amazing
World Record:** _____

SUPER SPOON-STICKER

You'll need spoons again for this one. How many spoons can you get to stick on your face at once? Try breathing on them to help them stick. Remember to wash them and put them away when you are finished!

First Attempt: _____

**My Amazing
World Record:** _____

PLAYGROUND GAMES

Those games you play at recess are about to get intense! Test your skills while setting new world records with these familiar objects.

HOOP IT UP!

What's your record for longest time you can keep a Hula-Hoop spinning around you? Once you are a hula expert, keep two spinning for as long as you can!

First Attempt: _____

**My Amazing
World Record:** _____

Transform your Hula-Hoop into a jump rope! How many times can you jump the hoop before missing?

First Attempt: _____

**My Amazing
World Record:** _____

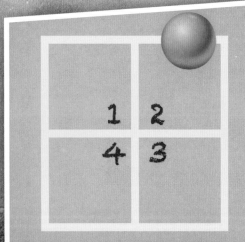

FOUR-SQUARE FOREVER

You need three friends for this one. Play Four-Square, but try not to get the other players out. How many hits can you make without a miss?

First Attempt: _____

**My Amazing
World Record:** _____

TITANIC TETHERBALL!

In tetherball, you usually try to beat your opponent. This time, work with a partner to see how many times you can knock the ball back and forth without missing.

First Attempt: _____

**My Amazing
World Record:** _____

★ Record to Beat! ★

According to Guinness World Records, Aaron Hibbs Hula-Hooped the longest. In a marathon session in 2009, he hooped for 74 hours and 54 minutes!

BUNNY BALL HOP

Put a kickball ball between your feet. Now see how far you can hop without losing the ball.

First Attempt: _____

**My Amazing
World Record:** _____

Now try it with a tennis ball! Think that's easy? Add another tennis ball!

First Attempt: _____

**My Amazing
World Record:** _____

Your Inner Artist

Be a great artist...using not only your hands, but also your feet or mouth! These challenges test your unique artistic skills!

CHALK LINE CHALLENGE

What is the longest line you can make outside with one piece of chalk? You can't take the chalk off the ground once you start.

First Attempt: _____

My Amazing World Record: _____

VANISHING ART

Get a piece of sidewalk chalk that is at least five inches long. How fast can you make it disappear by writing on the sidewalk?

First Attempt: _____

My Amazing World Record: _____

TOOTHY TALENT

Use a paintbrush or markers to create a rainbow. Easy, right? You have to do it holding the brush or marker in your teeth! How quickly can you paint the rainbow?

First Attempt: _____

My Amazing World Record: _____

Amazing Fact

In 2013, a painting was sold for a new all-time record. The work by Francis Bacon (yes...his real name!) sold for $142 million! Might make you pay more attention in art class, huh?

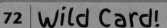

FOOT WRITING

How many three-letter words can you write holding a pen or pencil between your toes? See how many you can do in three minutes.

First Attempt: _____

**My Amazing
World Record:** _____

SUPER-DUPER CHALLENGE: FOOT FEATS

How talented are your feet? Writing is just one of the odd ways you can use your feet. We've thought of others. Practice these other fantastic foot feats and record the dates of your success:

	Date of My First Attempt	Date I Mastered the Skill
Hold a spoon. Can you feed yourself? That's cool, but GROSS!	_____	_____
Brush your hair— or your pet's hair!	_____	_____
Pick up pencils from the floor. Can you pick up two at a time?	_____	_____
Throw a small ball. Remember to record your distances!	_____	_____
Play "Mary Had a Little Lamb" on a piano.	_____	_____
Paint a picture.	_____	_____

RUBBER and String

You'll need rubber bands and a ball of string or twine for these challenges. Most also need a pair of scissors. Always ask a parent before borrowing or using objects from around the house!

CLIP AND SPELL

How fast can you cut short pieces of string and form them into the letters AMAZING ME?

First Attempt: _____

**My Amazing
World Record:** _____

Now take those same pieces of string and use them all to make your name. You have to use all the pieces!

First Attempt: _____

**My Amazing
World Record:** _____

SET A RECORD? KNOT!

How many knots can you tie in two feet of string? They must be next to each other so they can be counted!

First Attempt: _____

**My Amazing
World Record:** _____

HIDE THE LEAD!

Take a pencil that's at least six inches long. How fast can you wrap it in string so that you can't see any part of the pencil (including the ends)?

First Attempt: _____

**My Amazing
World Record:** _____

A HAND AND A BAND

How far can you shoot a rubber band using your hand? Try different band sizes to get the maximum distance! Never shoot a band at another person! Never shoot a rubber band at another person!

First Attempt: _____

My Amazing World Record: _____

SUPER CHALLENGE: RUBBER (BAND) BALL

This challenge could take a very long time. Collect all the rubber bands you can find and make a rubber-band ball. How big can you make it? Record your progress here:

_____

_____

_____

_____

_____

How high can your rubber-band ball bounce?

First Attempt: _____

My Amazing World Record: _____

Record to Beat!

A man named Joel Waul created the world's largest rubber-band ball. It weighs 9,032 pounds and stands almost seven feet tall.

Trivia Time!

So you think you know a lot of stuff, do you? Well, it's time to put that mighty brain to the test. Start thinking!

ANIMAL ALPHABET

How fast can you write an alphabetical list of animals from "A" to "Z"? Try it again without repeating any of the animals from the first list!

First Attempt: _____

**My Amazing
World Record:** _____

CRAZY FOR COUNTRIES

Repeat this challenge, but use the names of countries instead!

First Attempt: _____

**My Amazing
World Record:** _____

Amazing Fact

If you're counting countries and you get to 200, you went too far. According to the U.S. government, there are 195 countries in the world (as of 2013).

TEST YOUR KNOWLEDGE!

How many items in each of these categories can you say (with no repeats!) in one minute? You will need someone keeping count for you as you speak. You can also make these head-to-head challenges with your friends by writing your answers instead of saying them.

	First Attempt	**My Amazing World Record**
Species of birds	_____	_____
Names of your friends	_____	_____
Countries of the world	_____	_____
Words that start with "Q"	_____	_____
Words that start with "Z"	_____	_____
Types of dogs	_____	_____
Names of candy bars	_____	_____
Things that live underground	_____	_____
Names of flowers	_____	_____
Things you find in a classroom	_____	_____
Famous people in music	_____	_____
Books you have read (start with this one!)	_____	_____
Noises animals make	_____	_____
Things in the sky or in space	_____	_____
Famous buildings	_____	_____
Onomatopoeia* words	_____	_____
World languages	_____	_____
Types of sports	_____	_____
Types of musical instruments	_____	_____

*Great word, huh? It means the use of words that stand for sounds: "bang,""zip," "pow," "hiss," etc.

master Sculptor

Do you have what it takes to be a great sculptor? Maybe. But these challenges are all about setting records, not creating art!

POTATO PYRAMID

Next time you have mashed potatoes for dinner, try this! How fast can you make a potato pyramid that's at least three inches tall? Don't forget to eat your work when you're done!

First Attempt: _____

My Amazing World Record: _____

DRIBBLE IT

You will need a beach or sandbox for this one. What is the tallest drip castle you can build? To make one, take very wet sand in your fist, squeeze, and let it dribble out the bottom. Keep dribbling on the same spot to build your spire!

First Attempt: _____

My Amazing World Record: _____

FUN WITH FOIL

How quickly can you make a spider out of tin foil? It must have eight legs and stand tall enough so the body isn't touching the table.

First Attempt: _____

My Amazing World Record: _____

SUPER CHALLENGE: DOUGH PLAY

Play-Doh is not just for little kids! It's great for setting world records! Each of these challenges needs exactly one can of Play-Doh! For each, you MUST use the whole can.

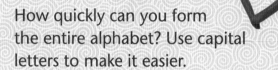

Make the longest snake you can. Your snake may be as thin as you want, but must not have any breaks!

First Attempt: _____

My Amazing World Record: _____

How many perfect snowmen can you make? Each must have three balls of different sizes and must stand on its own. They can be as big or small as you want.

First Attempt: _____

My Amazing World Record: _____

How many pretzels can you make?

First Attempt: _____

My Amazing World Record: _____

How quickly can you form the entire alphabet? Use capital letters to make it easier.

First Attempt: _____

My Amazing World Record: _____

Capitals too easy for you? Try sculpting all lowercase letters. What was your time?

First Attempt: _____

My Amazing World Record: _____

Amazing Fact

Mount Rushmore in South Dakota is one of the world's most famous sculptures. The creator, Gutzon Borglum, needed 14 years to complete the four-president masterpiece.

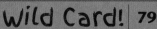

GOT A TOWEL?

For these challenges, water is your friend. (Making a huge mess, however, is not, so be chill...do these outside!)

FANCY FOOTWORK

You need lots of tinfoil balls about one inch across and two buckets. Place the buckets two feet apart and fill one bucket halfway with water. Place the tinfoil balls into the water. Using only your feet, transfer as many balls as you can into the other bucket in two minutes.

First Attempt: _____

My Amazing World Record: _____

TEETH TOTE

Fill a bucket with small water balloons and place an empty bucket 20 feet away. In three minutes, how many water balloons can you transfer from one bucket to the other using only your teeth? The ones that break in the bucket don't count!

First Attempt: _____

My Amazing World Record: _____

READY, AIM, SQUIRT!

Get a friend and a pair of squirt guns. Set up two identical glasses 10 feet away. Race to see who can fill up his glass the fastest, using only the squirt guns!

First Attempt: _____

My Amazing World Record: _____

WET HEAD

Get a plastic cup that holds about eight ounces. Fill it to the rim with water. Now see how far you can walk with the cup balanced on your head...without spilling!

First Attempt: _____

My Amazing World Record: _____

FRESH FROM THE WASHER

How fast can you put on a soaking-wet T-shirt?

First Attempt: _____

My Amazing World Record: _____

How about a wet T-shirt that has been left in the freezer overnight? Brrrrr.

First Attempt: _____

My Amazing World Record: _____

Want your friends to share in the fun? Have a frozen T-shirt available for each and see who can get dressed the fastest!

First Attempt: _____

My Amazing World Record: _____

Record to Beat!

In 2011, William Trubridge imitated a fish. Holding his breath, he dived 397 feet in just over four minutes to set a new free-dive world record.

FOOD FUN!

The coolest part about these challenges? You get to eat whatever you use to set the records! (Well, almost everything: Read the marshmallow one and make your own decision....)

ONE-HANDED CHEF

How fast can you make a peanut-butter-and-jelly sandwich on two pieces of bread... using only one hand? That includes opening the jars, spreading the stuff, cutting the bread...and cleaning up! For a bonus, try doing it with your "opposite" hand.

First Attempt: _____

**My Amazing
World Record:** _____

BANANA PEELER

How fast can you peel a banana using only your teeth? You can't use your hands in any way—including holding the banana!

First Attempt: _____

**My Amazing
World Record:** _____

Now how fast can you eat the banana? Remember...no hands!

First Attempt: _____

**My Amazing
World Record:** _____

SPIT-MALLOWS

You need mini marshmallows and a drinking straw for this challenge. Push a marshmallow onto one end of the straw. Now BLOW into the other end. How far did the marshmallow fly?

First Attempt: _____

**My Amazing
World Record:** _____

Amazing Fact

The farmers of two countries produce more than 80 percent of all the raisins in the world. Can you name them?

HOW DO YOU SPELL "RAISIN"?

For this challenge, you need a good-sized box of raisins. Pick up a magazine and randomly point to a word. Then see who can spell the word fastest using only raisins to form the letters on the counter.

First Attempt: _____

**My Amazing
World Record:** _____

Answer: United States and Turkey

KEEP 'EM SEPARATED

Get one cup each of peanuts, raisins, M&M's, and a Cheerios-like cereal. Mix all four cups together into one larger bowl. Time yourself to see how fast you can split the four foods back into their cups. No fair eating some to make it go faster!

First Attempt: _____

**My Amazing
World Record:** _____

THE GAMES OF GROSS!

Time to be disgusting and offend people around you. Awesome, right?

BRAAAPP!

What is the longest time you can do one continuous burp?

First Attempt: _____

My Amazing World Record: _____

What is the longest word you can burp-talk?

First Attempt: _____

My Amazing World Record: _____

How fast can you burp the alphabet?

First Attempt: _____

My Amazing World Record: _____

UNDERARM ORCHESTRA

What is the longest tune you can play with your armpit? Start with "Row, Row, Row Your Boat" and then try "Happy Birthday"!

First Attempt: _____

My Amazing World Record: _____

THE NOSE KNOWS

How fast can you blow up a balloon…using only your nose?

First Attempt: _____

**My Amazing
World Record:** _____

Amazing Fact

*The 2013 World
Watermelon Seed
Spitting Champion
was Oklahoma's
Darren Jennings.
He spit the pit 34 feet!*

PTOOEY!

How far can you spit a watermelon seed? (Hint: The black ones work best.)

First Attempt: _____

**My Amazing
World Record:** _____

How about a grape?

First Attempt: _____

**My Amazing
World Record:** _____

STRAW STRENGTH

First, the warm-up: You need two cups of the same size and a straw. Fill one cup with water. How fast can you empty one cup and fill the other just using the straw?

First Attempt: _____

**My Amazing
World Record:** _____

Now fill a cup with Jell-O. How fast can you transfer the Jell-O to the other cup using a straw?

First Attempt: _____

**My Amazing
World Record:** _____

Now to be truly gross: How about a cup of ketchup?

First Attempt: _____

**My Amazing
World Record:** _____

Random Acts!

We just didn't know where else to put these challenges, but we didn't want you to miss the chance to try them.

RAINBOW RUSH

In your home or classroom, find one object for each color: red, orange, yellow, green, blue, and purple. How fast can you find the rainbow?

First Attempt: _____

My Amazing World Record: _____

PERSONAL PUZZLE

Print out a picture of your face on a piece of copy paper. Then tear it into at least 24 pieces. How fast can you solve the jigsaw puzzle and put yourself back together?

First Attempt: _____

My Amazing World Record: _____

DICE & STEADY

Grab a Popsicle stick and five dice. Hold the Popsicle stick in your teeth. Carefully stack the dice on the very end of the stick. How long can you hold them there before they topple?

First Attempt: _____

My Amazing World Record: _____

MONEY ON THE MOVE

What's the longest time you can get a coin to spin before it's completely flat on the table?

First Attempt: _____

**My Amazing
World Record:** _____

★ **Record
to Beat!** ★

Chad Fell loves his bubble gum. In 2004, he set a world record by blowing a bubble that was 20 inches across. How big is that? A basketball is only 9 inches!

POP GOES THE RECORD

Time to chew for the gold! How many bubble-gum bubbles can you blow and pop in 30 seconds?

First Attempt: _____

**My Amazing
World Record:** _____

Construction Zone!

Put on your construction helmet and let's build! For these challenges, you'll need to make something that is really big, really tall, or really long.

SUPER STRAW

You'll need a box of straws—or two—for this challenge. What is the longest chain of straws you can make that you can still use to drink? No other materials allowed!

First Attempt: _____

**My Amazing
World Record:** _____

PRETZEL ARCHITECTURE

Make the tallest tower you can with 100 mini pretzel sticks and 50 mini marshmallows. How tall is your masterpiece?

First Attempt: _____

**My Amazing
World Record:** _____

Super Challenge: Add to your masterpiece. How tall can you make your tower with 300 pretzel sticks and 150 mini marshmallows?

First Attempt: _____

**My Amazing
World Record:** _____

ACE HIGH

What is the highest house of playing cards you can build? Take your time... and don't sneeze!

First Attempt: _____

My Amazing World Record: _____

COLOSSAL CUBE

A cube is the shape of a die: six sides of equal size. What's the biggest solid perfect cube you can make using only Lego or similar building bricks?

First Attempt: _____

My Amazing World Record: _____

RUBBER ROPE!

Love making things out of rubber bands? Try for the longest rubberband rope you can make! Knot them together as shown.

First Attempt: _____

My Amazing World Record: _____

Try this with your class and see how long you can make the rope in an entire school year!

Our Amazing World Record: _____

Small Is Big!

Adults might be bigger or stronger, but that doesn't mean they're better! See who can set the world record in these challenges—you or the people who used to be kids. Compete with an adult for each of these challenges!

WHO'S THE BETTER BOPPER?

Each challenger gets three balloons and must keep them all in the air for as long as possible. As soon as one balloon hits the floor, time's up! Who won? How long did he or she bop?

Best Bopper: _____

Time: _____

FINGER FRENZY

Put a half cup of dry rice on a large plate for each challenger. Then see who can move all that rice into a cup the fastest. Oh, wait. Did we mention you have to pick up one grain at a time with your fingers? Small fingers rule!

Fastest Fingers: _____

Time: _____

Amazing Fact

More than 90 percent of the world's rice is grown and eaten in Asia! There are more than 40,000 different types of rice grown around the world.

TOO-BIG DADDY

Kids have the advantage on this one: How much of yourself can you fit in a laundry basket?

First Attempt: _____

**My Amazing
World Record:** _____

NOSE BALL

Get a large package of cotton balls. Count them out into even piles. Then see who can move his or her pile into a bowl across the room the fastest. No hands, though. You have to pick up each cotton ball with your nose. Just breathe in…and hold it!

Winning Nose: _____

Time: _____

HOP TO IT

This challenge should make everyone hoppy! Who can jump rope on one foot the longest? If you don't have two ropes, time each other separately.

Who Won: _____

Time: _____

THAT'S JUST GROSS

After a good rain, head to a nice muddy field. Or try this at the beach at low tide. The object: Cover as much of yourself with mud or wet sand as you can. Who managed to get completely covered first? How long did it take?

Muddiest Member: _____

Time: _____

VISION QUEST

Ask your parents for a couple of empty pill bottles. Give each team one bottle. Now, without using glasses, who can find the letters "A" through "M" on the outside of the bottle the fastest. (Yes, grown-ups…those letters are pretty darned tiny!)

Who Spied the Fastest: _____

Time: _____

WHAT'S THAT CREAKING SOUND?

Put on some bouncy music and let's limbo! Who can limbo lower, the kids or the adults? How low did you go?

Who Limboed Lowest: _____

My Amazing World Record: _____

READY, SPAGHETTI

Who has steadier hands? For this test, you need a raw piece of spaghetti for each player and a small bowl of ring-shaped cereal. Using only one hand and the piece of spaghetti, who can stack five pieces of cereal first?

Super Stacker: _____

Time: _____

Record to Beat!

According to World Record Academy, Shemika Charles is the world limbo champ. She squeezed under a bar that was just 8.5 inches off the ground!

POLITENESS MARATHON

Perhaps this is the hardest challenge of all! Who can go the longest without yelling…about anything? Can you make it for a week? Longer?

Most Polite: _____

My Amazing World Record: _____

Bonus: Beat Your B

MY OWN WORLD RECORDS

We're not the only ones who can think up challenges. You can, too! You've seen how it works: You need something fun to do that can be measured and recorded. On this page, make a list of the challenges you and your friends make up and record the results. Have fun (and, since I'm a dad, I have to say this: be careful).

Challenge: _____

Results: _____

Challenge: _____

Results: _____

Challenge: _____

Results: _____

Challenge: _____

Results: _____

Challenge: _____

Results: _____

I'M AMAZING!

AMAZING ME!